EXTREME PHYSICS

KINGFISHER
NEW YORK

KINGFISHER
LONDON & NEW YORK

Text and design copyright © Toucan Books Ltd.
Based on an original concept by Toucan Books Ltd.
Illustrations copyright © Simon Basher 2013

Published in the United States by Kingfisher,
175 Fifth Ave., New York, NY 10010
Kingfisher is an imprint of Macmillan Children's Books, London.
All rights reserved.

Consultant: Professor James Valles

Designed and created by Basher www.basherbooks.com
Text written by Dan Green

Dedicated to Leigh Coleman

Distributed in the U.S. and Canada by Macmillan,
175 Fifth Ave., New York, NY 10010

Library of Congress Cataloging-in-Publication data has been applied for.

ISBN: 978-0-7534-6969-9

Kingfisher books are available for special promotions and premiums.
For details contact: Special Markets Department, Macmillan,
175 Fifth Ave., New York, NY 10010.

For more information, please visit www.kingfisherbooks.com

Printed in China
9 8 7 6 5 4 3 2 1
1TR/0413/UTD/WKT/128MA

CONTENTS

Introduction
Extreme Physics

When it comes to physics, things don't get much more extreme than the weird "quantum" stuff people like to talk about. This realm of miniscule things was discovered in the early 1900s by scientists who were on the hunt for teeny-weeny parts of matter. They had the idea that if they could track down the so-called fundamental particles— the parts from which all larger things are made—then they could explain the way everything works. Fat chance!

What they *did* find was so completely crazy and unexpected, it defied explanation! For particles have a tendency to pop up in two places at once and refuse to be measured. Eventually, supersmart Erwin Schrödinger (and others like him) found ways to use math to describe how these mini mischief-makers do their mind-bending tricks. And yet, unlike many larger systems, it remains almost impossible to predict what a quantum particle is going to do next. This wild, uncertain world is bursting with the fruit-loop-crazy characters you're about to meet. They don't have time for the rules of the ordinary world and seek only to blow your mind—you're gonna love them!

Erwin Schrödinger

Chapter 1
Quantum Folk

Loony, lively, and full of pep, the Quantum Folk are an unpredictable bunch! These guys like to make life difficult for people who want to find out how they work. The largest player in this quantum world is Atom—the foundation block of matter. Atom makes all that you can see around you, so if you understand this fellow, understanding the universe should come easy! However, it's when you start to unpack Atom to see how it is made that the mind-boggle begins. People call the quantum domain a "rabbit hole," because there's a zany Wonderland down there, just as there was when Alice fell down that hole!

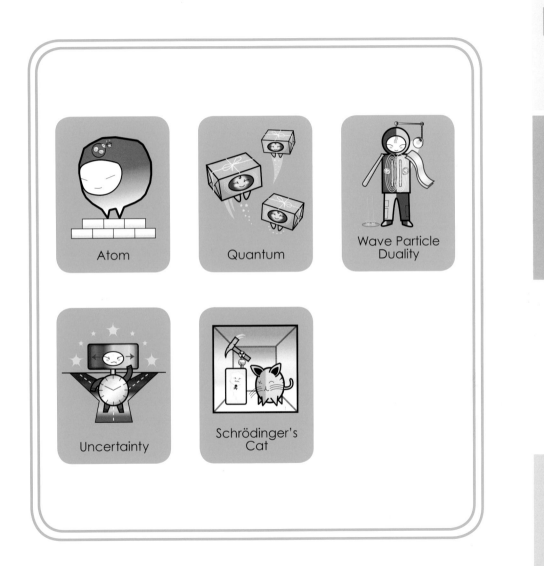

Atom

Quantum

Wave Particle Duality

Uncertainty

Schrödinger's Cat

Atom

◉ Quantum Folk

✳ The basic building block of all matter
✳ Made of protons, neutrons, and loosely held electrons
✳ Quantum effects prevent an atom from collapsing

I'm smaller than a pinprick—half a million of me could hide behind a single hair—but I'm the stuff that *matters*! You see, I make up every single thing around you—the gases you breathe and the things you chew or stub your toe on.

You might expect me to be solid, but I'm mostly empty space. Anything smaller than me is called "subatomic" (smaller than an atom), and it's at this level that quantum activity occurs. For example, 10,000 times smaller than me, and squashed into a tiny space at my core, is my nucleus. Home to the Particle Posse, this is where Proton and Neutron reside. Orbiting the nucleus is speedy Electron. Electromagnetic Force makes sure that Electron stays inside fixed energy levels, which are arranged around the nucleus a little like the layers of an onion.

● Discovery: 1803 (John Dalton, theory); 1905 (Albert Einstein, proof)
● Average size: 1×10^{-10} m (0.0000001 mm)
● Number of atoms in your body: about 10^{14} (100 billion billion)

Atom

9

Quantum

◉ Quantum Folk

☀ A parcel of light energy or subatomic particles
☀ Electrons in atoms can only occupy fixed energy levels
☀ Particles "leap" from one level to another

I'm a neat little package of matter or energy, and I come in a selection of fixed sizes. Later, when you meet the Particle Posse, you'll see that Photon is the *quantum* of light and Electron the *quantum* of electricity. But what does all of this mean, exactly?

Well, imagine you're riding a bike. Put some oomph into pedaling, and you go faster. More oomph and you go faster still. In theory, it seems that you can give your bike as much energy as your legs will provide. This is not so in the quantum world, however, where energy is "quantized" and comes in set amounts (quanta). For you on your bike, this means that only one set energy is allowed to move each gear cog. Atom's energy is quantized in this way to ensure that it is stable and doesn't collapse.

● Discovered: Max Planck (1900) and Albert Einstein (1905)
● Quantum radiation: energy given off in "lumps" from atoms
● Quantum absorption: energy absorbed by atoms in "lumps"

Quantum

Wave Particle Duality

◉ Quantum Folk

- ✺ All quantum objects are both particles and waves
- ✺ This duality was revealed by the "double-slit" experiment
- ✺ Matter and light can be described using "wave functions"

I am the enigma at the heart of the quantum world. I prove that, on teeny-weeny quantum scales, particles of matter and light lead double lives. Allow me to explain.

On the one hand, particles act like particles—compact objects like baseballs. But they also act like waves— rippling movements that carry energy. This discovery was the result of a mind-blowing experiment that showed what happened to particles when fired through two slits in a flat surface. Amazingly, the particles were seen to interfere with each other in the same way that water waves mingle when two stones are dropped side by side into a pool. Weirder still, a single particle fired at the same surface appeared to pass through both slits at once and so was effectively in two places at the same time. Wacky!

- ● Discovered: 1924 (Louis de Broglie, theory); 1927 (Davisson and Germer, proof)
- ● Wave functions: mathematical formulae that describe matter and light
- ● Wave function first formulated: 1926 (Erwin Schrödinger, Austria)

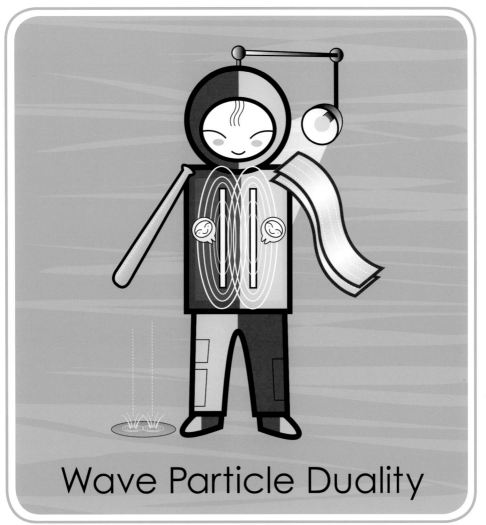

Wave Particle Duality

Uncertainty
◉ Quantum Folk

☀ A mathematical limit to the preciseness of quantum predictions
☀ Certainty in position leads to uncertainty in momentum . . .
☀ . . . and certainty in momentum leads to uncertainty in position

I'm the lack of certainty built into the most basic level of matter and physics. At any point in time, you can know where a particle *is* but not where it's *going*. At least I think that's how it works—I'm a little fuzzy on the details!

My vagueness has nothing to do with the difficulty of measuring these tiny quantum things. No, it has much more to do with my pal, Wave Particle Duality. You've seen how quantum particles have a waviness associated with them. Well, this wobbliness can be described using a mathematical equation called the wave function. And computing this wave function to find the position of, say, Electron gives you a "probability cloud" of possible locations. This is simply a measure of the likelihood of finding Electron at any given point in space. Now you see it . . .

● The uncertainty principle: 1927 (Werner Heisenberg, Germany)
● Electron orbital: region around an atom in which an electron is likely to be found
● Chance of locating the electron in the electron orbital: 90%

Uncertainty

Schrödinger's Cat

◉ Quantum Folk

☀ A "thought experiment" devised by physicist Erwin Schrödinger
☀ This cool cat explains the idea of "superpositions"
☀ Makes you ponder the weirdness of the quantum realm

I'm a kitty locked in a box with some radioactive gunk, a hammer, and a glass tube full of poison gas. Meow! If the radioactive particles decay, the hammer is triggered, swings, and smashes the glass tube. A *cat*-astrophe!

This imaginary set-up is designed to make you think. How can you know whether or not the gas is out? Simple— you open the box. But wait! Before the box is opened I could be alive or I could be dead, right? And if I were a subatomic particle (according to quantum mathematics, at least), I could also take a third, both-alive-and-dead state! Since each of these states is equally likely, I exist in a "superposition" of the three. Until you look in the box, that is, which "forces" reality to "choose" a single outcome. This paradox is a real case of curiosity killing the cat!

● The big idea: 1935 (Erwin Schrödinger, Austria)
● Deadly gas proposed for experiment: hydrocyanic acid
● Chance of radioactive alpha decay: 50%

Schrödinger's Cat

Chapter 2
Particle Posse

Meet the Particle Posse. These roughnecks can be found inside Atom—the building block of all matter (the stuff that takes up space). Matter that we encounter in our everyday lives is mainly made up of Proton, Neutron, Electron, and Quarks, but there are many other types of subatomic particles. The most basic are fundamental particles. Just like the heart of a Russian nesting doll (on a superteensy scale), these fellows cannot be split to reveal anything smaller. A theory called the Standard Model requires six Quarks and six leptons, plus a handful of force-carrying particles to keep it all together.

Quarks

◉ Particle Posse

✳ A bouncing bunch of fundamental particles
✳ These little tykes combine to form larger subatomic particles
✳ Bound together by gluons, quarks cannot be isolated

Meet the Quark family, but please say our name correctly—it rhymes with pork! Full of charm and a little strange, we are the top and bottom of everything.

We come in six different "flavors": Up, Down, Charm, Strange, Top, and Bottom. We exist at a deeply buried level of reality, huddled in the most cramped spaces in the universe. Found in groups, we combine to make particles of matter, such as Posse pals Proton and Neutron. But we're a bunch of tricksters and like to swap flavors. Heh heh! The heavier a Quark is, the less it likes to hang around. Top blinks out after just 0.4 million million million millionths of a second. Up and Down are the least heavy; this pair makes up most of everyday matter. You won't find anything purer than us—that's elementary!

● First quark discovered: bottom (1977, Fermilab, United States)
● Last quark discovered: top (1995, Fermilab, United States)
● Heaviest quark: top (35,000 times more massive than up or down)

Quarks

Proton
◉ Particle Posse

✳ Positively charged subatomic particle in the core of an atom
✳ This stable "baryon" is made of two up quarks and one down
✳ The number of protons present determines an atom's properties

Buried deep within Atom's nucleus, I'm so positively charged that I'm simply bursting to get out. I'm a big fellow—about 2,000 times heavier than my negative pal, Electron—but Strong Force and his Neutron police keep me locked up tight in here. Only a very small part of my mass is accounted for by my Quarks. The rest is pure, fizzing energy.

Proton

● Discovered: 1918 (Ernest Rutherford, United Kingdom)
● Charge of a proton: + 1.60217646 x 10^{-19} C (coulombs)
● Mass of a proton: 1.67262158 x 10^{-27}kg

Neutron
Particle Posse ◉

- A neutral subatomic particle in the core of an atom
- A baryon made up of two down quarks and one up
- Determines nuclear and radioactive properties of an atom

Neutron

Heavy, and perhaps a little stodgy, I am cooped up inside Atom's nucleus, where I keep boundlessly positive Proton in check. My neutrality means that only Strong Force and Gravity have the power to move me. When I break free from the nucleus, I get a chance to show my wild side, splitting radioactively to release an electron and an electron antineutrino.

- Discovered: 1932 (James Chadwick, United Kingdom)
- Charge of a neutron: zero
- Mass of a neutron: 1.674927351 x 10^{-27} kg

23

Electron
◉ Particle Posse

☀ Very light, negatively charged subatomic particle
☀ A sparky member of the lepton family and carrier of electricity
☀ An essential part of everyday matter

The elementary particle with all the best moves, I bring electricity into your home and do all the legwork inside your favorite gadgets. Call me King Lepton!

I zip around Atom's outer regions, orbiting so fast that I become a mere blur. My negative charge draws me to positive Proton—we're equal in number inside Atom—but I'm an independent soul and like to do my own thing. I can move freely between atoms; the moves I make determine the course of most chemical reactions. Scientists have long thought that I was fully fundamental—that is, with no smaller parts into which I could be broken—but when I get into Atom, interactions with other electrons can make me look like I'm splitting apart. Reality's Russian doll may yet reveal another secret . . .

● Discovered: 1897 (J. J. Thomson, United Kingdom)
● Charge of an electron: $1.60217646 \times 10^{-19}$ C (coulombs)
● Mass of an electron: $9.10938188 \times 10^{-31}$ kg

Electron

Muon
◉ Particle Posse

☀ Joins electron as a member of the lepton family
☀ This "heavy electron" is an unstable fundamental particle
☀ Negatively charged and relatively easy to detect

A weighty lepton, I blink in and out of existence in 2.2 microseconds. And believe me, in the pretty-darn-quick world of subatomic particles, that's an age. I'm produced when cosmic rays from outer space smash into molecules in Earth's upper atmosphere. I rain down in invisible showers, and about 100 of us are passing through your body at this very moment!

Muon

● Discovered: 1936 (Carl D. Anderson, United States)
● Charge of a muon: $1.60217646 \times 10^{-19}$ C (coulombs)
● A muon is 200 times heavier than an electron

✴ This scale-busting lepton is extremely unstable and short-lived
✴ Exists for mere trillionths of a second
✴ Carries the same charge as an electron

Named after the Greek letter "tau," I believe in living life to the full. (Well, when you exist for only trillionths of a second, you have to!) Like all fundamental particles, I have no internal structure—I'm complete and whole just as I am, thank you! I am affected by Weak Force and, because I'm charged, Electromagnetic Force.

● Discovered: between 1974 and 1977 (Martin Lewis Perl, United States)
● Charge of a tau: $1.60217646 \times 10^{-19}$ C (coulombs)
● A tau is almost 3,478 times heavier than an electron

Neutrino

◉ Particle Posse

✳ Ultra-lightweight subatomic particle from the lepton family
✳ Has three forms: electron, muon, and tau neutrinos
✳ Trillions of these flyweights are passing through you right now

Up, up, and away! I am a "neutral little one"—the tiniest bit of reality ever discovered. Thanks to an absence of electric charge, lack of weight, and the eyewatering speeds at which I travel, I am virtually undetectable.

I come blazing out of the Sun by the trillion every second, generated in nuclear reactions at its core—woo-hoo! I form when Neutron falls apart at the seams. Like all leptons, I am unaffected by Strong Force but, unlike negatively charged Electron, Muon, and Tau, I'm neutral. Because I don't have an electric charge, Electromagnetic Force can't touch me, and as I have virtually no mass, Gravity can't either. In fact, only Weak Force has an effect on me. This is how I managed to avoid all human surveillance systems until 1956, when I was caught exiting a nuclear reactor core.

● Discovered: 1956 (electron neutrino); 1962 (muon neutrino); 2000 (tau neutrino)
● Charge on all neutrinos: approximately zero
● Mass of a neutrino: approximately zero

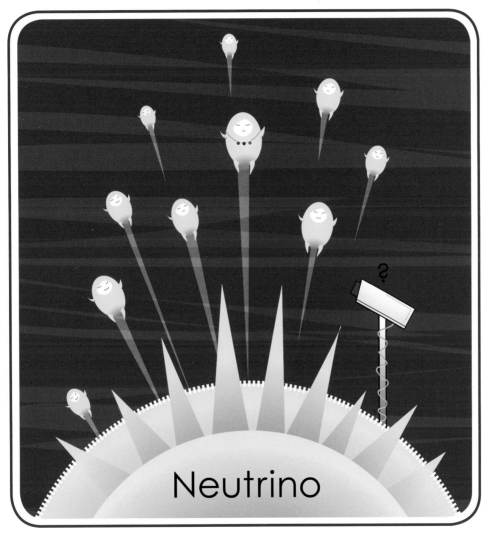

Neutrino

Photon

⊙ Particle Posse

❋ A massless, chargeless particle and the quantum of light
❋ Detected as radio waves, visible light, x-rays, and gamma rays
❋ The exchange particle for electromagnetic force

A ray of sunshine, I'm the only fundamental particle that humans can see. I zap across the vacuum of space at the speed of light, transporting the dazzle of the stars. I'm created by everyday electrical and chemical reactions such as fire. Atom releases me when Electron throws out excess energy. I'm also made when particles of matter meet Antiparticle.

Photon

● Discovered: 1905 (Albert Einstein, Germany); 1923 (Arthur Compton, United States)
● Mass and charge of a photon: zero
● Minimum number of photons needed for them to be visible: about 100

Gluon
Particle Posse ◉

* Gooey exchange particle that transmits strong force
* Binds quarks together in particles of matter
* Eight types of gluons exist, each one without mass or charge

Gluon

Strong and sticky, I'm the glue that gums Quarks to one another. Deep inside Atom's nucleus, I keep particles such as Proton and Neutron from falling apart. I use a property that physics geeks call "color" (which is nothing like the colors you might use to paint a picture). Although I'm extremely strong, I can only operate over very short distances.

● Discovered: 1978 (DORIS electron-positron collider, Germany)
● Charge of a gluon: zero
● Number of colors (types): 8

Weak Bosons

⊙ Particle Posse

✳ The exchange particles for weak force
✳ Unlike most force-carrying particles, they are high in mass
✳ The final word in force-carrying particles . . . as far as we know

Known as W^+, W^-, and Z^0, we are the messenger particles for Weak Force. Exchanging us allows the heavier Quarks and leptons to change "flavor" and become less massive. You could call us flavor enhancers! We also enable Proton to change to Neutron, a spicy transformation that makes the Sun shine. Savor the flavor!

Weak Bosons

● Discovered: 1983 (UA1 experiment, CERN, Switzerland)
● Lifespan of a weak boson: 10^{-25} seconds
● Z^0 is 90 times more massive than a proton; W^- and W^+ are 80 times more massive

Graviton
Particle Posse ◉

* As-yet undiscovered exchange particle for gravity
* Expected to be a massless and stable particle
* Predicted to travel at the speed of light

Graviton

I'm a poorly understood, shadowy particle, waiting in the wings while the world celebrates Higgs Boson. Hey, I might not even exist! Quantum physics has successfully used particles to explain the other three Fundamental Forces (you'll meet them later), so scientists think there must also be a particle for the final force, Gravity. It's an *attractive* theory . . .

● Discovered: undiscovered/theoretical
● Charge of a graviton: zero
● Mass of a graviton: zero

Higgs Boson

◉ Particle Posse

✳ Long-awaited particle, predicted by the Standard Model
✳ This heavy dude is the particle that gives mass to matter
✳ Massless particles are unaffected by Higgs Boson

I burst onto the scene in 2012 and am now as famous as a Hollywood A-lister. I eluded physicists for years, until they built the world's biggest particle accelerator—the LHC—to find me. When, after 45 years in hiding, I turned up and so proved my existence, it's no wonder they felt like partying!

I help to explain mass. Stuff made out of matter (everything you see around you) has mass, but where does it come from? Well, physicists think that I'm the answer. You see, I come from a field that spreads through all of space like a three-dimensional mist of invisible, sticky molasses. Honestly! I cluster around particles as they move through this field. Heavier particles pick up more of me, so they "experience" more mass and are slowed down more than other particles are. Sweet and dandy!

● Proposed by Peter Higgs (1964)
● Discovered: 2012 (CERN, Switzerland)
● *LHC* stands for Large Hadron Collider, built between 1998 and 2008 at CERN

Higgs Boson

Antiparticle

◉ Particle Posse

✳ An oppositely charged, mirror image of a matter particle
✳ Created in the lab in sprays of matter and antimatter pairs
✳ Found in small quantities (thankfully) in Earth's atmosphere

An evil twin, I have an identical mass to any particle, but the opposite charge. I am created in high-energy collisions whenever I meet my counterparticle of matter. The result is a flash of pure energy. Shake hands with your antimatter twin, and you'd both be destroyed in a catastrophic nuclear explosion! Boy, I give the universe a little *pizzazz*!

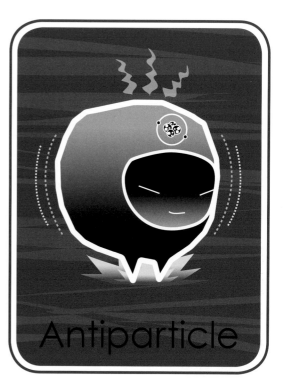

Antiparticle

● Discovered: 1932 (Carl D. Anderson, United States)
● Charge of an antiparticle: opposite to the charge of its counterparticle
● Mass of an antiparticle: equal to the mass of its counterparticle

Dark Matter

Particle Posse ◉

✴ A spooky kind of particle that is totally invisible
✴ This mystery of the universe neither emits nor absorbs light
✴ Has the ability to pass straight through normal matter

Dark Matter

I am Mr. Enigma, the strange, alien matter from which the universe is made. There's a lot of me around —five times as much as normal matter. Humans can detect normal matter because it absorbs and emits light, but no one has ever actually seen *me*! I make my presence felt via my gravitational attraction, which keeps galaxies spinning on their hubs.

● Dark energy makes up around 70% of the universe
● Dark matter makes up around 25% of the universe
● Normal matter makes up around 5% of the universe

Chapter 3
Fundamental Forces

Meet the four Fundamental Forces that rule the universe. Agents of change, these dynamic dudes shake things up and make things happen. Each one has its own sphere of operations: Weak Force plugs away inside subatomic particles such as Proton and Neutron; Strong Force works inside particles, too, but its effects are felt within Atom's nucleus; Electromagnetic Force is a player at the atomic and interatomic levels, and like Gravity, its effects are felt over huge distances. Some of these characters join forces at high energies, so physicists think that all four might, at some point, morph into one awesome superforce!

Weak Force

Strong Force

Electromagnetic
Force

Gravity

Weak Force

⦿ Fundamental Forces

- ☀ A short-range force that affects all quarks and leptons
- ☀ Can change a quark from one flavor (type) into another
- ☀ Has several force-exchange particles called Weak Bosons

Zap! Pow! I'm mini in strength, but maxi in effect. I'm a billion, trillion, trillion times stronger than Gravity—nothing puny in that, huh? Okay, I'm much weaker than Strong Force and Electromagnetic Force, but still I'm no wimp!

Just like my pal Strong Force, I do my work over teeny-weeny distances—mostly inside Atom's nucleus, where my force-carrying Weak Bosons make Quarks swap their flavors. Under my direction, for example, Weak Bosons change a Down Quark into an Up Quark (so that Neutron becomes Proton). This kind of nuclear decay changes Atom into a completely new element and releases a radioactive Electron. Similarly, when I change Proton into Neutron inside the Sun, this releases tons of energy and a flood of Neutrinos and keeps the Sun shining. Hot stuff!

- ● Discovered: 1968 (Glashow, Salam, and Weinberg, United States)
- ● Range: about 10^{-18}m (size of a quark)
- ● Best-known effect: radioactive beta decay

Weak Force

Strong Force
Fundamental Forces

※ The most powerful of the four fundamental forces
※ Holds the nucleus of an atom together
※ Causes nuclear explosions when it breaks down

El Strongo Magnifico, I am more than 100 times stronger than Electromagnetic Force and a million times tougher than Weak Force. I am the universe's circus strongman.

Inside Atom's nucleus, I do battle with Electromagnetic Force, who makes positively charged protons repel each other violently. I keep it all together—without me there'd be no Atom. My strength works over very short distances, which explains why you are blissfully unaware of me! As well as keeping Proton and Neutron tightly imprisoned inside Atom's nucleus, I act on the particles nested within them— the Quarks—who interact by exchanging my awesomely powerful Gluon particles. Every time they do so, they change their quantum state, or "color charge," and this whirlwind flashing keeps 'em attracted to each other.

● Discovered (in theory): 1934 (Hideki Yukawa, Japan)
● Range: 10^{-15}m; also 10^{-18}m
● Best-known effect: nuclear fission (nuclear bombs)

Strong Force

Electromagnetic Force
Fundamental Forces

✹ A force with infinite range that you can feel all around you
✹ Holds atoms together by attracting electrons to the nucleus
✹ Carried from place to place by photons

Bzzzrkt! Crackling with energy, I'm an electric character with a magnetic personality. Outside of the unthinkably small regions of Atom's nucleus, Strong Force and Weak Force are utterly powerless. *Mwa ha ha!*

I embody the rule that opposites attract. I cause attraction between oppositely charged particles and poles and repulsion between like-charged particles and poles. The force of attraction between electrons and protons holds atoms and molecules together and keeps your body from drifting apart. Repulsion between electrons on the outer regions of atoms and molecules stops your fingers from going through this book! I boss Electron around in electronic devices, bringing you phones and T.V., and I bring light into the world via my force-carrying particle, Photon. *Zap!*

● Discovered: 1820 (Hans Christian Oersted, Denmark)
● Range: infinite
● Best-known effect: electricity generation

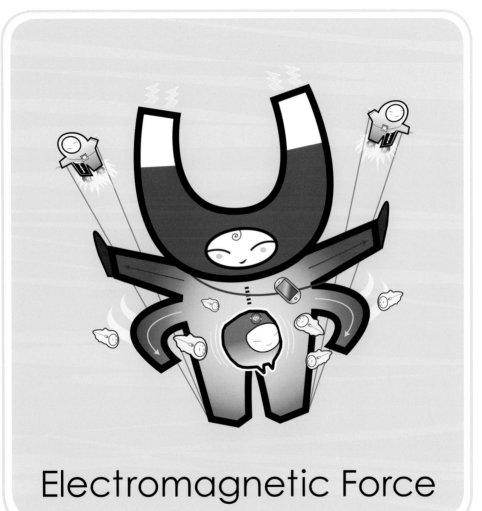

Electromagnetic Force

Gravity
Fundamental Forces

☀ A force of attraction felt between objects made of matter
☀ Keeps you drawn to the surface of Earth
☀ The weakest of the four forces yet infinite in range

I am a mystical mover and shaker and "fundamentally" different from the other three forces, ha ha! I keep planets in their orbits, help stars form, and make sure your feet stay on the ground. There's no floating around on my watch!

Any body that has mass—the mysterious property that all matter possesses—feels me. The more mass you have, the more you feel my pull and the heavier you are. You might think I am a straightforward, down-to-Earth force (geddit?), but quantum mechanics has trouble explaining me completely. For starters, I have almost no effect on subatomic particles. Plus, I only ever attract, never repel. And while I ought to have an exchange particle, like the other Fundamentals do, no one has seen or heard so much as a squeak from shadowy "Graviton."

● Discovered: 1666 (Isaac Newton, United Kingdom)
● Range: infinite
● Best-known effect: attraction of objects toward Earth's center

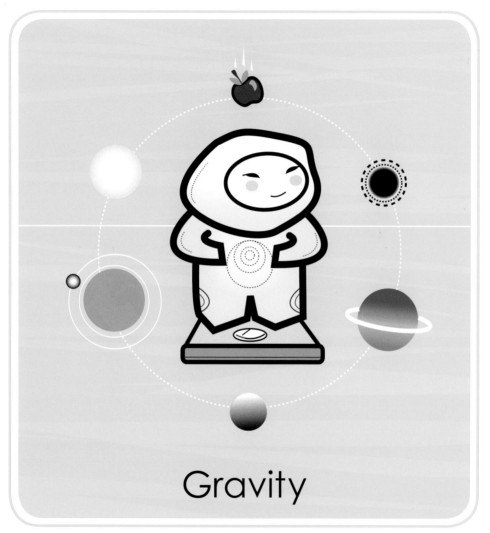

Gravity

Chapter 4
Quantum Weirdness

Matters are about to get *really* strange. Here, things blink in and out of existence like Cheshire cats; solid particles suddenly turn into wavy streaks of pure energy, and stuff doesn't even appear until it is measured. It's as if the act of lifting the lid on something *makes* it exist. But Quantum Weirdness is not beyond comprehension. Sure, it's tricky to make predictions about the behavior of individual quantum particles, but we *can* explain how they work as a crowd. In fact, microchips, LEDs, lasers, biotechnology, and superconductors all rely on this odd crew. So set your weird-o-meter to minus three and step over the threshold. *Wibble*!

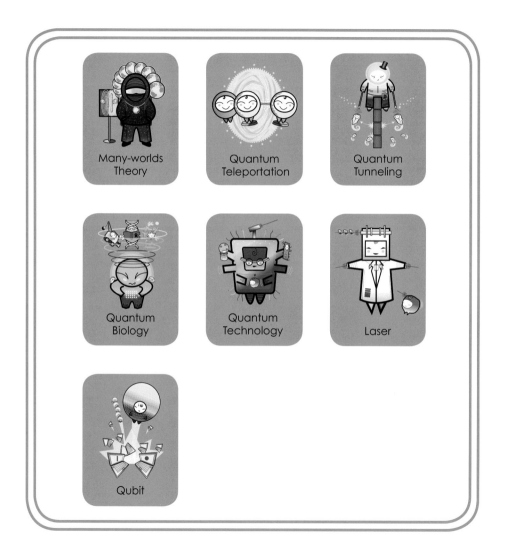

Many-worlds Theory

Quantum Teleportation

Quantum Tunneling

Quantum Biology

Quantum Technology

Laser

Qubit

Many-worlds Theory

◉ Quantum Weirdness

☀ Attempts to explain the results of the double-slit experiment
☀ Proposes the existence of parallel universes
☀ Challenges the "superpositions" of Schrödinger's Cat

I am a traveler from lands hidden, unknowable, and strange. I know things that you'll never know and, boy oh boy, I've seen things you'll never see.

You've already heard, from Wave Particle Duality, that particles have an uncanny habit of being in two places at once. Remember the double-slit experiment? Try watching closely to see how one particle can pass through two slits at the same time, and it doesn't happen. That's right! The act of looking seems to collapse the magic and you see the particle pass through only one slit. In fact, something truly mind-blowing is happening, because the particle *does* go through the other slit. It's just that this happens in a "parallel universe"—a similar, but disconnected, world that you'll never be able to visit. Shame!

● The big idea: 1957 (Hugh Everett, United States)
● Number of "MEs" writing this: infinite
● Number of "YOUs" reading it: infinite

Many-worlds Theory

Quantum Teleportation
Quantum Weirdness

✴ Works using "entangled" particles
✴ Where a given measurement of one particle affects another
✴ Changes occur no matter how far apart the particles are

I am the future, my friend. I create "terrible-twin" quantum particles and use them to zap information around the universe in an instant. I may be another crazy prediction from the equations of quantum mechanics, but have no doubt—people will be using my magic in years to come. Beam me up, Scotty!

When two particles are created at the same time, their properties become "entangled"—they buddy up. Give one buddy particle new information by making it interact with a third particle, and identical changes instantly occur to its partner—even with the distance of the entire universe between them! So far, my spooky magic works only on things that are smaller than a molecule, so don't expect to see humans transported around *just* yet.

● The big idea: 1935 (Albert Einstein, Boris Podolsky, and Nathan Rosen)
● Entanglement record: 89 mi. (143km) (Canary Islands, 2012)
● Largest entangled particle: 0.000001mm ("buckyball")

Quantum Teleportation

Quantum Tunneling

◉ Quantum Weirdness

✳ This magician transfers electrons through walls in an instant
✳ Relies on the built-in probabilistic nature of "wavy particles"
✳ Particles are said to "borrow energy from the future"

Jeepers creepers, I'm a quantum leaper! There's just no confining me. My Houdini-like talents allow members of the Particle Posse to pass straight through walls and appear unharmed on the other side.

Thanks to my pal Uncertainty, quantum particles don't ever have a fixed position in space (unlike baseballs and birds). This means that, for any barrier that keeps, say, Electron in one place, there is a small chance it could be found on the other side of it. In other words, it can exist on both sides at once. Sounds crazy, but it gives me a role in all kinds of important functions. I trigger the Sun's nuclear fusion reaction and get to work inside the most high-tech touchscreens. I may even be able to influence the delicate workings of biological life processes.

● Discovered: 1927 (Friedrich Hund, Germany)
● Typical barrier size: 1–3nm (0.000001–0.000003mm)
● Tunnel diode invented: 1957 (Leo Esaki, Japan)

Quantum Tunneling

Quantum Biology
◉ Quantum Weirdness

✸ Powers living things on the most basic level
✸ Provides essential life services for both plants and animals
✸ Operates on the tiniest scales of electrons and protons

Lean and green, I use the power of the quantum realm to organize and run affairs inside cells. I take charge of the way cells exchange gases with the outside environment. I drive photosynthesis in plants and make sure biochemical reactions go supersmoothly for enzymes. You've got it— I am Nature's very own nanotechnician!

Quantum Biology

● The big idea: 1944 (Erwin Schrödinger, Austria)
● Could explain how some birds navigate by sensing Earth's magnetic field
● Average size of a cell: 0.01–0.03mm (animal); 0.01–0.1mm (plant)

Quantum Technology

Quantum Weirdness

☀ Involves busy quantum effects within subatomic machinery
☀ Operates lasers, superconductors, and semiconductors
☀ Works on the tiny scale of atoms and electrons

Quantum Technology

I'm at the heart of the latest gadgets—you'll be amazed where you can find me. Quantum know-how has led to the development of the microchip, LEDs, and other semiconductor technologies in electronic devices. I can provide crisp pictures of your insides, while my atomic force microscope (AFM) can now image atoms directly.

● Discovery of superconductivity: 1911 (Heike Kamerlingh Onnes, the Netherlands)
● First commercial LEDs: 1962
● Invention of the AFM: 1986 (Binnig, Quate, and Gerber, Switzerland)

Laser
◎ Quantum Weirdness

✳ Quantum device that produces light of a single frequency
✳ Works on the principle of quantized energy levels within atoms
✳ LASER = Light Amplification by Stimulated Emission of Radiation

Highly honed and finely toned, I make "light" work of any task. The light I produce is genuinely of a higher caliber than that of any ordinary light source. My product is strictly "monochromatic"—of one frequency and color—and "coherent"—all the photons in a beam are in step.

I'm 100 percent quantum. I work on the principle that Electron—in orbit around Atom—absorbs only a fixed amount of energy to leap up to a higher energy level. When it falls back, it releases this quantum of energy as a photon of light. Because the frequency of light is related to its energy, the same transition always gives off the same frequency (or color) of light. You'll know me as a reader of digital data on DVDs and bar codes, but I'm also used in quantum experiments for trapping and chilling Atom. Cool, huh?

● The big idea: 1916 (Albert Einstein)
● First working laser: 1960 (Theodore Maiman, United States)
● Temperature of steel-cutting laser: 9,000°F (5,000°C)

Laser

Qubit
⊙ Quantum Weirdness

✳ The smallest possible piece of quantum information
✳ A bunch of these little bundles makes a quantum computer
✳ Multiple qubits entangle to make a calculation

Welcome to your future! You're looking at the Next-Gen of superbad computers, built around tiny packets of quantum information. I can inhabit Atom, Electron, or even Photon, and I'm set to turn the world on its head!

Your computer crawls along using run-of-the-mill "bits" of information that can only ever be in one state—either a 1 or a 0. Well, I can be a 1 or a 0, too. But, true to my Quantum Weirdness ways, I can also be somewhere in the middle or *both* at the same time! You could say I'm a little like Schrödinger's Cat. I double the options for each bit and when I become entangled with another qubit, my processing power becomes squared! Futurists predict that I'll create truly intelligent machines one day. And by the way, my name is pronounced "Q-bit," not "kwi-bit," okay?

● The big idea: 1982 (Richard Feynman, United States)
● Time a fast computer takes to factorize 1,000-digit number: 10 million, billion, billion years
● Time a quantum computer takes to factorize 1,000-digit number: 20 minutes

Qubit

Glossary

Baryon A subatomic particle made of three quarks, one of each color (red, green, and blue). Protons and neutrons are baryons.

Charge A property of matter that describes how strongly it is affected by electromagnetic force.

Color A property that describes how quarks interact via strong force.

Composite particle A subatomic particle that is made up of two or more other subatomic particles—for example, baryons. Because they can be split into simpler components, composite particles are not elementary.

Elementary particle Also called a "fundamental particle," this is a part of matter that cannot be broken down into anything smaller or simpler.

Entanglement Also called "quantum entanglement," this is a phenomenon where two particles (that interact with each other) can affect each other, even when they are separated by huge distances.

Enzyme A special protein made by the body. Chemical reactions influenced by enzymes require less energy to kick-start and go millions of times quicker.

Exchange particle Also called a "gauge boson," this special "force-carrying" particle is exchanged between particles, allowing them to "feel" forces.

Flavor The six different types of quarks are called flavors. Weak force can change a quark from one flavor to another.

Interatomic The term for interactions that occur in the spaces between atoms.

Lepton A member of a family of fundamental particles that includes electrons and neutrinos. Leptons are affected by weak force.

Mass A property of matter that describes how strongly it is affected by the force of gravity.

Matter The stuff that makes up the world around us—the things that we can touch, smell, and see. Matter is made up of atoms, which in turn are made up of smaller, elementary subatomic particles.

Microsecond One millionth of a second.

Molecule A small piece of matter made of two or more atoms bonded together by electromagnetic force.

Momentum A measure of the "oomph" that a traveling body, such as a particle, has. A particle's momentum is its mass multiplied by its speed.

Negatively/positively charged Electric charge comes in two types— positive and negative. The two are attracted toward each other.

Neutral Having no charge. A neutral particle does not interact with, and is not affected by, electromagnetic force.

Nuclear Anything that goes on inside an atom's nucleus, or any interaction that involves the nucleus of an atom.

Nucleus The central part of an atom, made up of protons and—in all elements apart from hydrogen—neutrons.

Paradox A puzzle in which the pieces don't seem to fit together, or in which the answer seems to contain a contradiction.

Photosynthesis The process by which plants convert energy from the Sun into food that their cells can use.

Probability cloud In quantum mechanics, the position of a particle cannot be determined precisely. Instead there is a "fuzzy region" of places, inside which there is a chance that it might turn up—that region is a probability cloud.

Quantum interference All waves can collide and become mixed up with one another. Quantum interference is the name given to this occurrence when it happens with subatomic particles, owing to their wavelike nature.

Radioactive Describes an unstable substance with an atomic nucleus that breaks down and releases nuclear radiation.

Semiconductor A material that conducts electricity better than an insulator, but not as well as a metal (conductor). Such materials are used for controlling electric currents inside electronic devices and are the "brains" of all computers.

Spin A property of subatomic particles that is a little like the momentum an object picks up when it rotates. Spin can take only certain fixed values.

Stable Any molecule, atom, particle, or system that is not likely to change physically or chemically or decay radioactively.

Standard Model The complete theory that describes all subatomic particles and the forces that act upon them.

Subatomic particle Anything that is smaller than an atom.

Superconductor A material with zero resistance to electrical currents. It can make a megastrong magnet, but needs to be extremely cold to work.

Superposition When two or more things happen in the same place; the principle that particles can exist in several different quantum states at once.

Unstable The opposite of stable. A molecule, atom, particle, or system that is likely to change or decay (break down) without warning.

Index

Pages that show characters are in **bold**